26.95 n.ol.

CONSERVING THE ATMOSPHERE

John Baines

Conserving Our World

Acid Rain
Conserving Rainforests
Waste and Recycling
Conserving the Atmosphere
Protecting Wildlife
The Spread of Deserts

Cover: The atmosphere surrounds the
Earth, protecting it and supporting all
life forms.

Series editor: Sue Hadden
Series designer: Ross George

First published in 1989 by
Wayland (Publishers) Ltd
61 Western Road, Hove
East Sussex BN3 1JD, England

Second impression 1990

**British Library Cataloguing in
Publication Data**
Baines, John
  Conserving the Atmosphere.
  1. Air Pollution.
  I. Title II. Series.
  628.5'3.

ISBN 1 85210 696 4

Typeset by L. George and R. Gibbs,
Wayland.
Printed in Italy by G. Canale & C.S.p.A.

Contents

What scientists, weather forecasters, aeroplane pilots and other experts call the 'atmosphere', most people know as the 'air'. Neither of these two words adequately describes what the air is or what it does. Even a scientific description gives us only a partial understanding of what the atmosphere means to us.

The atmosphere plays a large part in our daily lives but most of the time we do not stop to think about it. We notice brilliant sunshine, sheeting rain, strong winds or snow, but we rarely pause to think about the atmospheric conditions that cause them.

Authors and poets use descriptions of the atmosphere to match the mood of their literature.

People can make use of the atmosphere for sports, such as hang-gliding.

When an electrical charge forks from a storm cloud down to earth, it creates some spectacular effects, which we call lightning.

It may be 'the stillness of the night air', 'the raging of a storm' or 'the enchantment of a sunset'. Film producers use storms, winds, thunder and lightning to add extra drama to a particularly tense or frightening scene. Painters and photographers of landscapes use dramatic skies to set a mood for their pictures. We even use the word atmosphere to describe the feelings we have about a place. A school which is enjoyed by its pupils is said to have a happy atmosphere.

The air around us is more than just a mixture of gases, water and dirt. It provides the oxygen necessary for us to survive, although we usually do not even notice that we are breathing. If we have a headache or need to think about a problem, a walk in the fresh air can make us feel much better. Of course, the atmosphere does not just support us – it gives life to all the plants and animals that share the earth with us. Therefore it is very precious and we should learn to value it.

In this book we shall take a close look at what the atmosphere is and how it supports life on earth. We will also think about how our activities are changing the atmosphere and the dangers that arise from this. Finally, we will examine what is being done, and what still needs to be done, to ensure that the atmosphere remains in good condition for the future.

What does the atmosphere do?

The atmosphere is made up of a mixture of gases, water vapour, dust and dirt. It surrounds and protects the earth from bombardment by meteorites and harmful radiation. It supports life. Without it, the earth would be as barren as the moon – no oceans, no rivers, no lakes, no plants, no animals, no you.

This alpine meadow is full of flowers, thanks to the atmosphere that surrounds our planet.

The gases that make up the atmosphere are invisible, but water vapour can be seen where it has made clouds. This picture, taken 37,000 km above the Earth, shows the continents of Africa and Antarctica very clearly.

*The diagram **below** shows the different gas layers that make up the Earth's atmosphere.*

The layers of the Earth's atmosphere

Height above sea level (in km)

Exosphere about 500km
Outermost layer of Earth's atmosphere.

Ionosphere about 60km
Layer with very high temperatures. Electrically charged particles called ions move freely around.

Stratosphere about 40km
Cloud-free layer at a constant temperature.

Tropopause (boundary of Troposphere)

Troposphere
This varies daily from a maximum of about 18km over the Equator to about 6km at the poles. All our weather conditions occur within this zone.

0

Nitrogen a JUST. EARTH. ON TRASD.

In the lowe   the main
gases are   ), oxygen
(almost 2   including
carbon dioxide,   nd krypton
(all together less than one   Within that
one per cent are now a number of new
human-made gases, some of which are highly
poisonous, such as dioxin.

The amount of each gas is very important. If
the level of oxygen dropped significantly, then
animals would not be able to breathe. If it was
much higher, the whole planet would be in
danger of catching alight. Even the miniscule
amounts of trace gases are very important. Each
one plays a vital part in protecting life on earth.

Water vapour

The atmosphere absorbs energy from the sun and from the surface of the earth. Where the air is warmest, it rises. Cool air comes in to take its place, creating winds. The air absorbs moisture from the sea, rivers, lakes, vegetation and the soil. This becomes water vapour in the air and can be carried hundreds of kilometres in the wind before returning to earth as rain or snow. These movements are so regular that it is possible to divide the world into climatic zones.

The balance of nature

The ingredients of the atmosphere have been held in balance for millions of years, but pollution by human activity is upsetting this balance and creating many problems. The atmosphere is getting too warm, the protective ozone layer is being destroyed, acid rain is damaging lakes and forests, and dangerous chemicals are poisoning people, plants and animals.

Conserving the atmosphere has become a major concern, not only for conservationists, but also for politicians, industrialists, farmers and the international community as a whole.

Winds are the movement of the atmosphere. They follow regular patterns, as shown in the map. The names reflect their importance to the early trading ships.

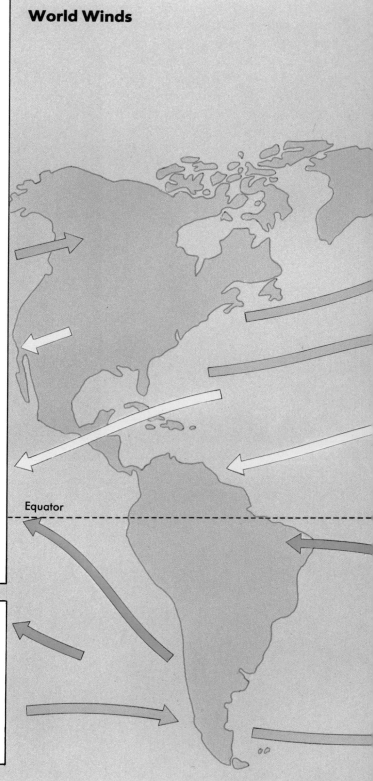

World Winds

Equator

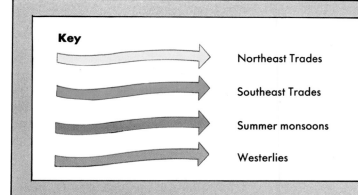

Key

Northeast Trades

Southeast Trades

Summer monsoons

Westerlies

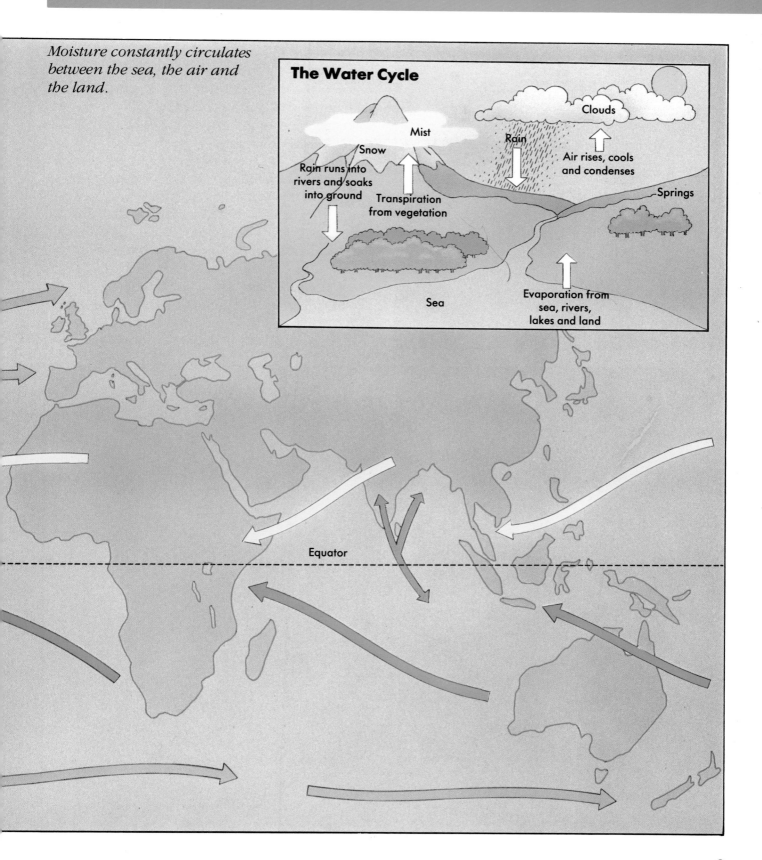

Moisture constantly circulates between the sea, the air and the land.

The Water Cycle

Clouds

Mist

Rain

Snow

Air rises, cools and condenses

Rain runs into rivers and soaks into ground

Transpiration from vegetation

Springs

Sea

Evaporation from sea, rivers, lakes and land

Equator

Fossil fuels and the atmosphere

Thirty years ago few people thought pollution could become a problem which would affect the whole planet. We now know that pollution is damaging the earth's climatic and ecological systems. One of the major causes of pollution is the burning of fossil fuels such as oil, coal and natural gas. These fuels are used to generate electricity, to make metals out of ores, to make chemicals, to heat homes, offices and factories and to power vehicles. When the fuels are burnt, the waste products are released through chimneys or exhaust pipes to pollute the air.

*Fossil fuels like coal produce smoke which can pollute the atmosphere (**left**). However, much of what appears to be pollution is water vapour from cooling towers at power stations (**below**).*

In the 1950s, storms and high tides coincided to flood low-lying areas of south-east England. In the 1980s a barrage was built across the River Thames to protect London from flooding. As sea levels rise, the barrier will be used more often.

Global warming

The temperature of the earth today is at its highest recorded level. Since 1900 it has risen by 0.5 °C, and a rise of another 1.5 °C is inevitable in the next fifty years. This may not seem much, and some people might even think it is a trend to be encouraged. However, since the last ice age, some 10,000 years ago, the world's temperature has risen by only 4 °C.

No one can predict the precise effect of such a rapid warming, but it is a question that world scientists have addressed. Their alarming predictions are as follows:

Rise in sea level

During the earth's history there have been many changes in the sea level. It was much lower during the ice ages when more water was held frozen in glaciers and ice sheets. Today, higher temperatures are causing more of the ice to melt and the sea level is rising. Since 1900, the level has risen by 10 to 15 cm, and by the middle of the next century it could rise by a further metre or more. This is sufficient to put large areas of coastal or tidal cities like New York and London at risk of regular flooding, and also to flood much of the best low-lying agricultural areas. In Bangladesh where the River Ganges reaches the sea, 15 million people could lose their homes. In prosperous Western countries, there is money available to improve sea defences, but developing countries are likely to suffer more frequent flooding.

This photograph from a satellite shows Hurricane Gilbert which caused terrible damage in many Caribbean countries in 1988.

Opposite Global warming may cause more floods in cities at or near sea level, like Calcutta .

More extreme weather patterns

Over the last twenty years, the weather over the world has become more extreme and many scientists attribute this to global warming. In Britain in 1987 and 1988 there were two storms in which the strongest winds for 250 years were recorded. Hurricanes in the Caribbean and the South Pacific are becoming more destructive and there have been devastating droughts in Africa, Australia and the USA. Such events do occur naturally from time to time, but freak conditions are causing them more and more often.

The major climatic zones will move

This will be most noticeable outside the tropics and will affect some of the most fertile and productive agricultural areas. Was the serious drought in the mid-west of the USA in 1988 an isolated freak, or was it a sign of things to come? Agriculture in other countries, including Canada and the USSR, will probably benefit.

*Strong winds are extremely powerful. In October 1987, record high winds blew down over half a million trees in southern Britain and caused great damage to houses and cars (**left**). In 1988, Hurricane Gilbert caused chaos in Jamaica, even throwing aeroplanes around (**below**).*

You have just read that global warming may cause the sea level to rise, more extreme weather patterns and a shift of climatic zones. Predictions are not always reliable, but there is agreement that the earth is warming and that this will affect the climate. This in itself is a problem. For example, major developments using water, such as hydroelectric power stations and irrigation schemes, rely upon accurate predictions of the climate. These are based on climatic statistics from the past. In 1985, an international

Central USA, one of the world's major cereal-producing areas, suffered a catastrophic drought in 1988. This crop of maize has hardly grown, although with normal rainfall it would be a metre high. Many American farmers suffered great losses as a result of this drought.

conference in Austria concluded that such climatic data was no longer a reliable guide. What do the planners use now to help them design new schemes?

The 'greenhouse' effect

Some of the gases in the atmosphere are known as 'greenhouse' gases. The heat of the sun can penetrate the gases, but its escape is slowed down. Without these gases, the world would be about 40° C cooler – too cold for life. If the gases increase, then not enough heat would be able to escape, and the world would become too hot to inhabit.

Although about thirty 'greenhouse' gases are known, 40 per cent of the global warming is caused by one gas – carbon dioxide. It is one of the gases formed when fossil fuels are burnt. The amounts found in the atmosphere are very small,

*The diagram **below** shows how carbon is released into the atmosphere.*

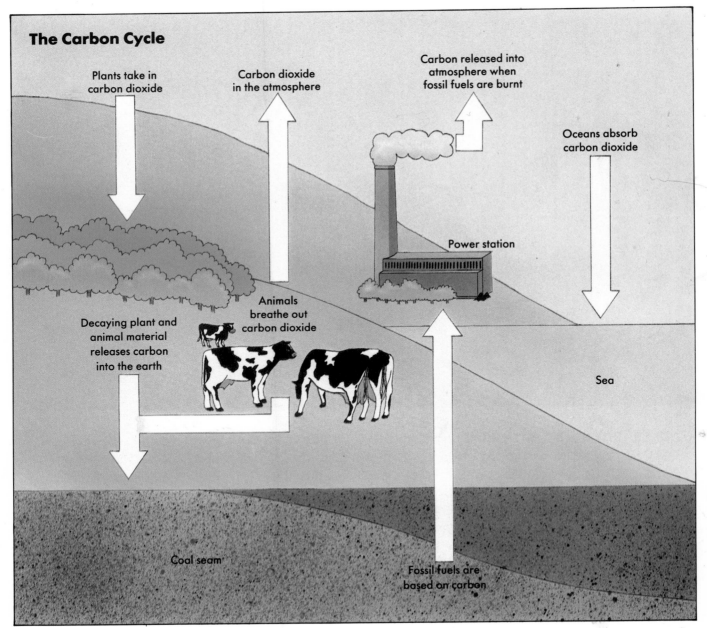

The Carbon Cycle

Plants take in carbon dioxide

Carbon dioxide in the atmosphere

Carbon released into atmosphere when fossil fuels are burnt

Oceans absorb carbon dioxide

Power station

Animals breathe out carbon dioxide

Decaying plant and animal material releases carbon into the earth

Sea

Coal seam

Fossil fuels are based on carbon

How the 'Greenhouse' Effect works

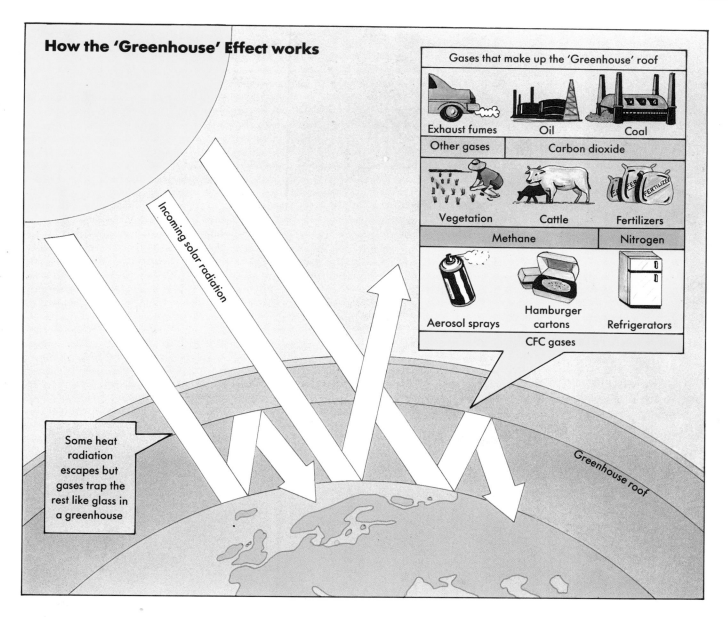

Incoming solar radiation

Some heat radiation escapes but gases trap the rest like glass in a greenhouse

Greenhouse roof

Gases that make up the 'Greenhouse' roof

Exhaust fumes	Oil	Coal
Other gases	Carbon dioxide	
Vegetation	Cattle	Fertilizers
Methane		Nitrogen
Aerosol sprays	Hamburger cartons	Refrigerators
CFC gases		

but are rising dangerously fast. In 1850, for every million litres of air, there were 265 litres of carbon dioxide (usually expressed as 265 parts per million). By 1958 the level had risen to 315 parts per million and in 1988 the figure had reached 350. As the levels rise, the 'greenhouse' effect worsens. As the temperature rises, more water evaporates and becomes water vapour in the atmosphere. The water vapour is even more effective than carbon dioxide in preventing the earth's heat from escaping. The effects of this are

*The diagram **above** illustrates how the 'greenhouse' effect works. Carbon dioxide causes 40% of the 'greenhouse' problem. Cutting down our use of fossil fuels and saving the world's forests can stop the problem getting worse.*

not felt immediately because it takes many years for the land, oceans and atmosphere to heat up. However, most scientists consider that a further rise in temperature of 1.5 °C is inevitable over the next fifty years.

Left It is hard to imagine that even grazing cattle can contribute to the 'greenhouse' effect, but cows are known to produce much methane.

The diagram **below** predicts the effect on global warming by various greenhouse gases.

Another 'greenhouse' gas that is causing concern is methane. The amount in the atmosphere is increasing at the rate of one to two per cent per year. It comes mainly from rotting vegetation in swamps and paddy fields, and from the mining and distribution of fossil fuels. Cattle also release methane when they are ruminating. In addition, methane slows down the rate at which the atmosphere can clean itself of other pollutants, such as sulphur dioxide. This is a major cause of acid rain.

Acid rain

Acid rain is causing great damage to lakes, rivers and forests in many parts of the world, especially Canada, the USA, Scandinavia and the mainland of Europe.

Sulphur dioxide and nitrogen oxides, formed when fossil fuels are burnt, are two of the main culprits. Water vapour in the atmosphere absorbs these chemicals and becomes a weak solution of sulphuric and nitric acids. This eventually reaches the ground as rain, snow or mist, and is thus known as acid rain. Throughout Britain the rainfall is ten times more acidic than is normal.

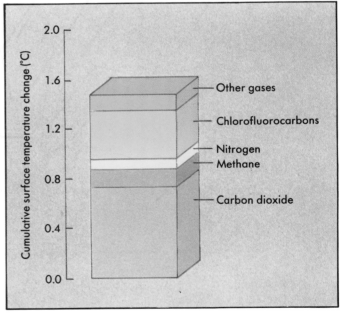

Some rain is so polluted that it is 1,000 times more acidic than normal.

The atmosphere is never still, as air moves vertically and horizontally. Pollution is carried in the air, sometimes for a week or more before it finally returns to earth. The damage it eventually causes may therefore occur a long way from the original source of the pollution.

Fishing is a popular pastime but it may be threatened, as many fish are becoming casualties of acid rain.

Damage to lakes and trees

One of the worst-affected areas in Europe is Scandinavia. The pollution is carried there from the major industrial areas of Britain, Eastern Europe and West Germany. Norway receives about 200,000 tonnes of sulphur in the air from other European countries every year. Canada claims that 50 per cent of the sulphur dioxide it receives comes from the USA. The first sign of the problem in Norway was that many lakes were losing their fish. Some seemed to have none at all. When this was investigated, it was noted that all the lakes had high acid levels. For a lake to remain healthy, it needs a pH of around 6.5. In some of the cases investigated, the pH had dropped to 4.5; a level at which the lakes could not support life at all. The main culprit was found to be sulphur dioxide, carried into Norway by the wind from other countries.

It was not until the 1960s that it was noticed that acid rain was also damaging trees and forests. Coniferous trees are the worst affected. The tops of the trees are the first to suffer, as they lose the needles which use the sunlight to grow. Where the pollution is more severe, needles are also lost lower down the tree. Eventually the tree becomes so weak that it is attacked by insects and fungi and dies. In the hills of Czechoslovakia, the damage is so severe that whole areas once forested are now treeless moorland. Damage to coniferous and deciduous trees has now been found in areas not thought to be at risk.

Other damage

Many buildings in or near industrial areas are showing the effects of acid rain. The stone decorations on some historic buildings have been dissolved by acid rain so much that they are unrecognizable.

People are also at risk if they eat certain foods.

Fish from acid lakes sometimes contain poisonous metals that have been dissolved out of the soil. The livers of moose, a delicacy in Scandinavia, are also often contaminated with these metals.

Above *These dying trees in North Carolina, USA, are showing the effects of acid rain.*

Below *The stonework of the remains of the Parthenon in Athens is deteriorating very rapidly because of acid rain.*

Vehicles and the atmosphere

There are about 550 million vehicles in the world today, enough to make a line of traffic long enough to stretch around the world about forty times. Of all forms of transport, cars and lorries cause the most pollution. We have already seen that vehicle exhaust fumes contribute both to acid rain and to the build-up of carbon dioxide in the atmosphere.

Petrol engines pump a number of harmful gases into the air. Carbon monoxide interferes with the supply of oxygen to the brain and can

Petrol engines pump a number of harmful gases into the atmosphere at street level, where they are inhaled by people. Leaded petrol is especially harmful to children.

lead to dizziness and headaches. Hydrocarbons (unburnt fuel) and nitrogen oxides react with sunlight to form ozone, which collects near the ground in traffic smogs. Such smogs are widespread in the USA and Europe. They can irritate the eyes and lungs, damage crops and corrode many materials. The USA blames 3,000 deaths a year on air pollution.

In many countries, petrol also contains lead, which ends up in the atmosphere. It is poisonous and can cause brain damage or behavioural problems in young children.

Diesel engines power most large vehicles like buses and lorries. They are also becoming more popular in cars. They use less fuel, but if they are not tuned properly, they can create a lot of black smoke and soot. It is suspected that this can cause cancer in some people.

The pollution from exhausts is particularly bad in towns and cities, where vehicles are jammed together in great numbers on tightly-packed networks of roads, hemmed in by buildings.

Of all forms of transport, vehicles cause the most pollution. Traffic jams, like this one in Bangkok, are a feature of cities around the world.

Along the streets the air can be very unpleasant to breathe and, along the busiest ones, it is positively harmful. The effects of pollution spread far from the towns and the highways carrying vehicles between them. In Switzerland, for example, the forests that protect villages and popular ski slopes from avalanches of snow, are being killed by traffic fumes.

Vehicles have a bad environmental record. None of the pollution they cause is necessary.

Cleaning up fossil fuels

There is only one real solution to the pollution caused by fossil fuels: clean up the atmosphere. Although we can filter pollution out of the air we breathe inside buildings, outside the only way is to stop the pollution from getting into the air in the first place. We have the technology to do this, but it is expensive and some say the costs are greater than the benefits. Pollution caused by burning fossil fuels can be reduced in a number of ways:

Using less fuel

Our way of life in the industrialized world is dependent upon using vast quantities of energy.

Fossil fuels are responsible for producing most of the energy we need.

We are learning to use fuel more efficiently, but a lot is still wasted. Heat escapes from badly insulated buildings, power stations put warm cooling water into rivers and the sea instead of re-using it, lorries return empty after delivering their loads and many of us are reluctant to leave our cars at home and use public transport instead. It has been estimated that we could use 50 per cent less fuel and still enjoy the same standard of living as we do today, if more energy conservation measures were introduced.

*The diagram **below** shows that public transport is an efficient means of travel. It is also much better for the environment.*

Vehicles and Atmosphere

		Number of kilometres per person
	A small car can carry one person for 9km on 1 litre of fuel	9
	4 people in a small car	36
	A bus with 40 passengers carries each person the equivalent of 50km on 1 litre of fuel	50
	A train carries each person the equivalent of 55km on 1 litre of fuel	55

Using less polluting fuels

Some fuels cause less pollution than petrol or diesel oil. Brazil has to import most of its oil and so, to save money, alcohol is being used instead of petrol. It is made from sugar cane and cassava. The exhaust fumes are almost clean enough to breathe. Brazil has also experimented with the use of vegetable oils to power diesel engines. These also cause much less pollution.

The atmosphere itself contains abundant energy. The wind is used to drive ships and windmills. Experiments are now taking place to use windmills to generate electricity. Waves are formed by the wind and they too can be used to generate electricity. Photo-electric cells use the energy directly from the sun to make electricity. Nuclear power is often proposed as a clean replacement for fossil fuels, but there is a lot of opposition to it because it is potentially so dangerous.

In Brazil, cars are fuelled by alcohol made from farm crops such as sugar cane and cassava. This non-polluting fuel is obtained from a pump, just like petrol.

Cleaning up the pollution at source

It is possible to prevent pollution entering the atmosphere. The smoke from power stations can have its sulphur dioxide content removed before it reaches the atmosphere. Cars can be fitted with catalytic converters so that the harmful carbon monoxide, nitrogen oxides and hydrocarbons are converted into less harmful carbon dioxide and water. But there is a cost. Our electricity bill could go up by as much as 10 per cent, and the cost of a car by between 3 and 5 per cent. This is not a very high price to pay for a clean and healthy environment, and it is certainly cheaper and better than damaged forests, crumbling buildings and poor health.

Stop the destruction of forests

Forests take in carbon dioxide and help control the amount of carbon dioxide in the atmosphere, reducing the 'greenhouse' effect. The huge areas of tropical forests in South America, Africa and South-east Asia are particularly important, but they are being removed very rapidly. As well as trying to reduce the amount of forest that is chopped down, we need to plant more forests. Gregg Marland of the Tennessee Institute for Energy estimates that to clean the atmosphere of the 5 billion tonnes of carbon dioxide created each year by burning fossil fuels, 700 million hectares (an area 14 times the size of France) of new forests are needed.

Above *The huge tropical rainforests of the world are disappearing rapidly.*

Much of the cleared wood from tropical rainforests is burnt to form charcoal. The burning adds to the amount of carbon dioxide in the atmosphere.

25

International co-operation

A lot is being done to reduce the pollution caused by burning fossil fuels, but it is still not enough. Research in Scandinavia shows that we will have to reduce the amount of sulphur dioxide and nitrogen oxides in the atmosphere by 80 per cent to ensure a healthy environment.

Over the last ten years Europe has reduced the amount of sulphur dioxide pumped into the atmosphere by 25 per cent. Over the next ten years it will be reduced by a further 30 per cent, thanks to more efficient use of fossil fuels and pollution control. Countries are showing that they are willing to co-operate with each other to solve the problem. In 1979, thirty countries signed an agreement to reduce their emissions of sulphur dioxide. In 1985 they fixed a reduction

Pollution of the atmosphere is an international problem. Members of the United Nations regularly meet together to reach solutions.

An important step towards cleaning up the atmosphere is to raise public awareness of pollution. Here two Greenpeace campaigners display a banner in central London.

of 30 per cent as their goal, creating what has become known as the '30 per cent Club'. There are now attempts to get similar agreements for nitrogen oxides, but nothing so far to reduce the amount of carbon dioxide.

To understand the scale of the problem and the solutions needed, more information is required. In 1980 the United Nations set up the Global Environmental Monitoring System which now has 175 sites in forty-two countries monitoring the state of the atmosphere. All the data is collected centrally to enable a global picture to be drawn.

The United Nations also runs an education programme. This aims to tell people about the state of the environment, what needs to be done to protect it and what is being done by nations individually and in co-operation with each other.

Clean exhausts are possible

The pollution from vehicles in cities such as Los Angeles and Tokyo became so severe that people decided they would no longer tolerate it. Very strict laws now make it illegal for any vehicle to exceed certain levels of pollution. The laws are so strict that one European car, on average, puts out as much nitrogen oxide as twelve vehicles in California.

The most successful way of reducing pollution from petrol-engined cars is to fit a catalytic converter. This is a small device fitted into the exhaust of the car. It converts 90 per cent of the harmful hydrocarbons, nitrogen oxides and carbon monoxide into less harmful carbon dioxide, nitrogen and water. It will work effectively only if unleaded petrol is used. As a result unleaded petrol is most popular where the exhaust emission controls are strictest.

In February 1989, the Queen delighted British environmentalists by announcing that her fleet of cars would all be converted to run on lead-free petrol.

Lead in petrol

Lead is added to petrol to improve an engine's performance. But lead is poisonous and highly dangerous for young children as it can damage the development of the brain. It can also cause them to be abnormally active and aggressive.

There is now a move in most countries to reduce or remove lead in petrol. For example, in Britain the amount of lead in petrol has been reduced from 0.4 to 0.15 grammes per litre. As a result, the amount of lead in the air over the whole country has reduced from 7,300 to 2,900 tonnes. In West Germany, the use of lead in petrol was banned in 1988.

Most cars will run on lead-free petrol without any modification to the engine. Most others require only a cheap modification. Despite lead-free petrol being cheaper in Britain than normal petrol, only one driver in a thousand was using it at the start of 1988.

The benefits of using lead-free petrol are:

- Less pollution, especially if cars are also fitted with a catalytic converter.

- Lower fuel bills. Lead-free petrol is often cheaper and the cars also use less fuel.

- Engines, exhausts and engine oil last longer, reducing the cost of regular maintenance.

As lead-free petrol becomes more widely available, more motorists are using it.

How to reduce exhaust pollution

- Better technology. Scientists have developed 'lean burn' engines. These use more oxygen so that the fuel is burnt completely and causes less pollution.

- Regular maintenance. A well-tuned engine produces less pollution.

- Driving smoothly. Rapid acceleration uses a lot of fuel and increases pollution.

- Driving more slowly. A car travelling at 140 kph produces twice the nitrogen oxides per kilometre as one travelling at 70 kph.

- Checking tyre pressures. Soft tyres create more resistance and therefore more petrol is used, but it is dangerous to pump in too much air.

- Whenever possible use public transport, cycle or walk. The last two are pollution free and are healthy.

The ozone layer

Ozone is a form of oxygen that is found in very small quantities in the upper atmosphere. Between 17 and 21 km above the surface of the earth it is concentrated in a narrow layer only a few Kilometres thick. This layer is very important to life on earth because it filters out 99 per cent of the sun's ultraviolet radiation, which would otherwise damage plants and animals.

The importance of this ozone layer has been known about for a long time. Since the 1950s it has been monitored by the British Antarctic Survey in Antarctica. Little attention was paid to

this data until the 1980s when it was discovered that, year after year, the amount of ozone in the upper atmosphere over Antarctica was getting less and less. In fact, during the winter of 1987, a huge hole as large as the USA developed in the ozone layer. The findings were confirmed by a weather satellite which had also been monitoring

This photograph, taken in 1986 from the satellite NIMBUS-7, shows the extent of the ozone hole over Antarctica. The hole is shown by the areas of grey. During the winter of 1988, it was reported that the hole extended as far as South Island, New Zealand.

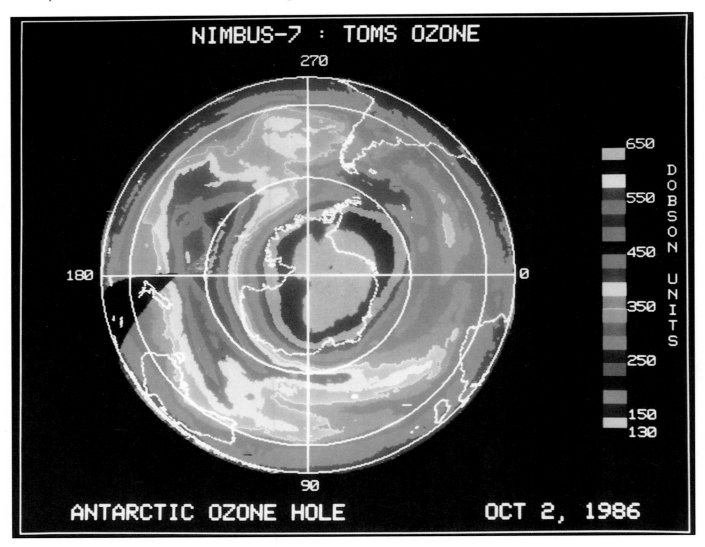

The ozone layer protects us from the sun's harmful ultraviolet radiation. If it is damaged, some fair-skinned sunbathers will increase the risk of getting skin cancer. These bathers are on Philips Island beach, Australia.

the ozone layer for years, but because no one believed it was important, the computer analysing the data had been programmed to ignore it. By chance, the world had discovered the beginnings of an environmental disaster.

The size of the hole varies according to the seasons. Although there is evidence that the ozone layer over the North pole is also affected, the destruction has not yet spread to the atmosphere above the middle and lower latitudes where most people, plants and animals live.

Ultraviolet radiation

Even a one per cent increase in ultraviolet radiation can damage living things. If this happened, it is estimated that there would be 15,000 new cases of skin cancer in the USA, as well as an increase in the number of eye cataracts, which severely limit a person's sight. Plankton in the oceans supports marine life. It is very sensitive to ultraviolet radiation and, if it is damaged, could upset all life in the oceans. But this damage may be minor in comparison to the damage caused to DNA molecules. DNA carries the instructions to cells that determine the physical development of plants and animals. If the DNA molecules are damaged, then we can only guess at what could happen to living things.

The ozone layer also absorbs heat from the sun, warming the upper atmosphere. The less the amount of ozone, the less heat is absorbed. In turn this would lead to a change in the world's wind patterns which would cause changes to the climate and weather experienced at the surface. We have already seen that the heating of the earth through the 'greenhouse' effect would also lead to changes in the climate and weather.

Chlorofluorocarbons (CFCs)

The damage to the ozone layer is caused by a group of chemicals that are known as chlorofluorocarbons, or CFCs. They have many useful properties. For example they do not affect

*The diagram **below** illustrates that CFCs are responsible for the damage to the ozone layer.*

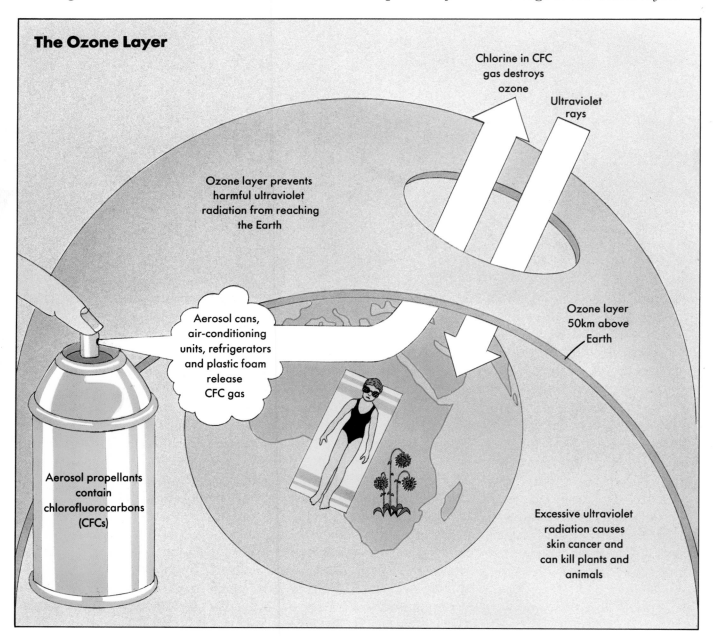

The Ozone Layer

Chlorine in CFC gas destroys ozone

Ultraviolet rays

Ozone layer prevents harmful ultraviolet radiation from reaching the Earth

Ozone layer 50km above Earth

Aerosol cans, air-conditioning units, refrigerators and plastic foam release CFC gas

Aerosol propellants contain chlorofluorocarbons (CFCs)

Excessive ultraviolet radiation causes skin cancer and can kill plants and animals

Left Today most households have a refrigerator and freezer. However, these contain a coolant that damages the ozone layer.

Below CFCs in aerosols have been banned in the USA since the 1970s. Now in many countries aerosol manufacturers are avoiding using CFCs. When buying a canister, look to see if it has an ozone-friendly sticker.

liquids. They do not change their colour or smell and they are not poisonous. They are perfect for using in aerosols to propel liquids through a nozzle in a fine spray and are used almost universally. Other uses of CFCs include cleaning microchips and circuit boards in the electronic industry and blowing styrofoam cartons in which much fast food, such as hamburgers, is served.

One CFC called freon is particularly damaging to the ozone layer. It is used as the coolant in refrigerators. When the refrigerator is scrapped, the freon is released into the atmosphere.

Action to solve the problem

Even if all CFCs were banned today, it would take fifty years for the ozone layer to return to normal. The seriousness of the problem can be judged by the speed at which action has been taken by the international community.

Montreal Convention: In 1987 the world's first treaty to limit CFCs was signed by twenty-seven nations, including the major industrial nations. They have agreed to reduce consumption of CFCs by 50 per cent before 1990. However, this is not sufficient to solve the problem. Anything less than an 85 per cent reduction is unlikely to prevent the problem becoming worse. Many governments and industries have responded to pressure for stronger controls. As a result, the British government expects to reach the agreed reduction by 1989.

Finding substitutes: Before CFCs can be removed from the environment, scientists must find substitutes for them or alternative ways of doing the jobs CFCs do. There are substitutes that can be used in aerosols, and they have been used in the USA since the 1970s. Many industries are now using them and labelling those products as 'ozone friendly'. A firm in Florida, USA, claims to have developed an alternative for the electronics industry to use. The big US electronics company AT&T is using it and has already reduced its consumption of CFCs by 33 per cent. More fast food companies are now using packaging that does not use CFCs in its manufacture.

Research: Now that the extent of the problem has been realized, it has prompted much more research into substitutes for CFCs and into monitoring the quality of the atmosphere in general.

The outlook

The measures that are being taken to reduce the amount of CFCs in the atmosphere are very encouraging. They show what can be done and how quickly we can respond to environmental problems when consumers, governments and industry work together to solve a problem. However, we must not think the problem is totally solved. We still have a long way to go before we can reduce the amount of CFCs by the required 85 per cent. If we do achieve this reduction, it will indicate a positive change in our attitude towards the atmosphere.

Right The world's worst chemical accident occurred at Bhopal, India, in 1984. Following an explosion at the Union Carbide factory, a cloud of poisonous gas engulfed the surrounding area. Two thousand people died, along with much of their livestock. Thousands of the survivors will suffer health problems for the rest of their lives.

Disposing of chemical waste

Chemicals are an important part of our lives. They are designed for many purposes from killing pests in agriculture to cleaning microchips used in computers. Many of them are extremely dangerous and, once used, are difficult to dispose of. There are very strict controls on their use and disposal in most industrialized nations, but sometimes the controls are ignored or there is an accident. When this happens, dangerous fumes can be released into the atmosphere and breathed in by people.

Burning toxic waste

To make poisonous chemical wastes safe, they have to be burnt at a very high temperature. One of the most dangerous groups of chemicals to living things are PCBs. They are so dangerous that it is illegal in Europe to find any new uses for them. However 200,000 tonnes will still have to be disposed of, probably by burning, when out-of-date electrical equipment in which they were used is scrapped. They must be burnt at 2000 °C for a least 22 seconds to be made safe. Failure to do this means that very poisonous fumes are released into the atmosphere. These include dioxin, which is the most poisonous chemical known.

The process of burning wastes is known as incineration. Because there is a danger of incinerators causing air pollution, they have been built on ships so that the burning can take place at sea. Greenpeace is one environmental group that has campaigned against this, pointing to the accumulation of dangerous wastes in the sea near the burning areas and proving that one ship was actually releasing dioxin into the atmosphere.

Dangerous chemicals can be disposed of safely if they are burnt at very high temperatures. Special incineration ships burn waste at sea, where the controls are not so strict as on the land. However, whether burnt on land or at sea, such chemicals still pollute the atmosphere.

Pressure from environmental groups like Greenpeace and Friends of the Earth is one of the reasons why the London Dumping Convention agreed that burning wastes at sea should stop in 1994. Sixty-five nations have signed the agreement, and have also agreed not to export the waste to countries that have not signed the agreement. The Association of Maritime Incinerators, which has invested a lot of money in three special incineration ships, claims that such a ban is unnecessary. In 1992, it intends to produce scientific evidence that burning is safe and should be allowed to continue.

Although dangerous chemical wastes are also incinerated on land, most land-based incinerators

To draw people's attention to the risks involved in burning dangerous waste at sea, the environmental group, Greenpeace, stormed an incineration ship in the North Sea and tied this banner around the chimney. Largely as a result of action like this, sixty-five nations have agreed to ban ocean incineration by 1994.

burn domestic, hospital and other wastes. Domestic waste presents a special problem, because it contains all kinds of rubbish, some of which may release dangerous fumes into the atmosphere when burnt. The same is true of garden bonfires if they are also used to burn household waste.

Right Roof timbers are often treated with chemicals to prevent woodworm and dry rot. However, the chemical fumes can kill birds and bats that might be living there.

Below We can all help the environment by taking old paints, engine oil and other chemicals to waste centres, where they can be disposed of safely. Never pour them down the sink or drain.

Controlling pollution

Dangerous chemicals can escape into the atmosphere in many ways, so control is extremely difficult. Agricultural sprays can drift in the wind and damage hedges, trees, garden plants and wildlife close by. Containers may leak, causing dangerous fumes to escape into the atmosphere. The fumes from wood preservatives used to protect timbers in the roof of a house may kill bats and birds, as well as the insects and fungi they are designed to kill.

Aware of the dangers, most countries have developed strict controls on the handling, use and disposal of chemicals and chemical waste. However, enforcing the controls is a great problem, leaving scope for the careless and the unscrupulous to pollute the atmosphere.

There is probably no form of pollution that generates as much fear as radioactivity. Unlike many forms of air pollution, it cannot be seen or smelt. Its effects on living things are not always predictable and may take many years to develop.

We are already exposed to radioactivity, more commonly known as radiation, which comes from outer space or seeps out of the ground. Of all the radiation we receive, 87 per cent is natural. The rest comes mainly from medical sources.

Nuclear power

Nuclear power is a very controversial issue. A nuclear power station uses fuel that is highly radioactive and produces radioactive waste. Great care is taken to prevent any radioactivity escaping into the atmosphere. Those who favour

*All forms of energy have advantages and disadvantages, as shown **below.***

Energy Sources	Cost	Benefit
Coal/oil fired power station	Causes acid rain. Adds to global warming. Loss of land to mining.	Pollution can be controlled at a cost. Power station covers small land area.
Wind power	Can spoil landscape. Noisy. Large area of land needed.	No pollution. Fuel (wind) is free.
Hydroelectric power	Floods large areas of land, destroying the original habitat.	Creates new habitat for water creatures. No air pollution.
Wave power	Possible danger to shipping. Covers large area of sea.	Little building on land needed. No air pollution.
Nuclear power	Produces radioactive waste. Risk of harming environment if radioactivity leaks.	No air pollution unless radioactivity leaks. Power station covers small land area.
Solar energy	Requires large area of land for solar panels.	No air pollution. Renewable free energy source.

nuclear power point out that it does not produce waste gases that contribute to the warming of the atmosphere or acid rain. It is 'environment friendly'. Those who oppose it point to the slight increase in background levels of radiation, the problem of disposing of radioactive waste and the possibility of a terrible accident releasing radioactivity into the atmosphere. The explosion at Chernobyl in the USSR provides the evidence that nuclear power is not safe.

The impact of Chernobyl

The accident occurred at a nuclear power station in a sparsely-populated area of the USSR near Kiev in 1986. Only two people were killed by the explosion itself, but others died over the following weeks of radiation sickness because they were exposed to high levels of radioactivity. Thousands of other Soviet citizens will probably never know whether they have been affected.

The impact of the explosion was not restricted to the immediate area. A huge invisible cloud of radioactive gases escaped into the atmosphere and was blown by the wind over the surrounding countries. In Germany whole areas of food crops were contaminated and had to be destroyed. Animals grazing in areas where radioactive rain fell were found to be unsuitable for human consumption, and farmers had to rely on government support to stay in business. Even in 1988, some hill farmers in Britain are still unable to sell their sheep. It may be thirty years before the traces of radioactivity disappear.

Nuclear power stations

Around the world there are about 350 nuclear reactors. When they are working normally, they are an expensive but clean way of producing electricity. However, when they go wrong they have the potential to pollute the atmosphere in the most dangerous way. For many people the risks are too great to compensate for the benefits. In the USA, no new nuclear reactor has been commissioned since the serious accident at Three Mile Island in 1979. Sweden has voted to phase out nuclear power when its twelve stations have ended their useful life. Britain and France, on the other hand, are committed to expanding the number of nuclear power stations.

In Britain, NIREX is responsible for finding a safe site for dumping nuclear waste, but few people want it to be near where they live.

Chernobyl nuclear power station, photographed after the 1986 accident which had such disastrous consequences.

Other forms of pollution

The indoor atmosphere

Pollution is not just restricted to the air we breathe when we go outside. The atmosphere inside our homes may also be polluted. There are many causes of this pollution.

If central heating boilers, water heaters, open fires and cookers using oil, solid fuel or gas are badly maintained, they will use fuel inefficiently and cause more pollution. They can also give off dangerous fumes such as carbon monoxide.

In our attempts to conserve energy during winter, it is common to keep windows closed and to block up cracks that might cause a draught. There may be insufficient ventilation in a room and the air can become very stale. If someone is smoking, or there is an open fire, then the air can become very polluted.

Increasingly, smoking is becoming a controversial issue. Medical research has proved that cigarette smoke harms not only the smoker, but non-smokers who inhale it.

Our kitchen cupboards, bathrooms, bedrooms and garages are full of chemicals that we use without a second thought: bleaches, cleaning fluids, glues, polishes and deodorants. Yet many of them pollute the atmosphere every time they are used. Just because it smells nice does not necessarily mean it is good for you.

Below right Smoking damages your health, but even non-smokers are at risk if they spend much time in a smoky atmosphere. Now there are a growing number of areas for non-smokers on public transport and in restaurants.

Below Many household products can pollute the air indoors if not used properly. Always keep them well sealed and follow carefully the instructions for their use and disposal.

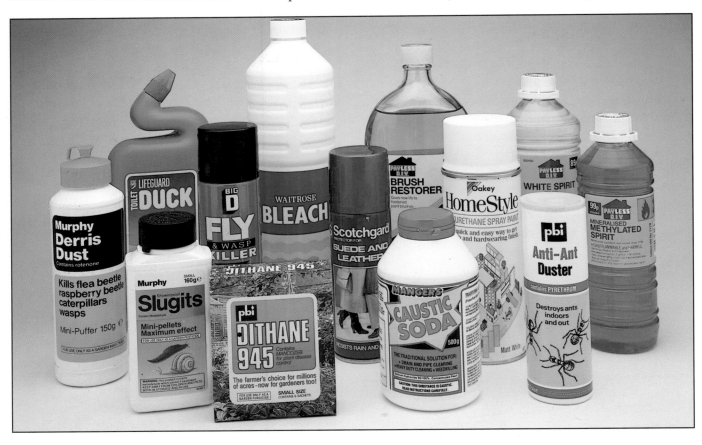

Noise in the atmosphere

Older jet aircraft can be very noisy. Jet engines used in newer passenger planes are designed to be much quieter.

One form of atmospheric pollution is very different from those already mentioned. A noise that one person considers pleasant, such as loud music at a party, another living next door may find very annoying. Noise can be dangerous. The vibration from heavy traffic can damage buildings close by. If people are exposed to loud noises for long periods, this can permanently damage hearing. For example, soldiers and people who often use guns may find a partial loss of hearing in the ear closest to the gun. Noise is becoming more of an environmental issue as people are becoming much less tolerant of unacceptable noise levels.

What else have we learnt?

Los Angeles is famous for its haze caused by pollution. These smogs are becoming rarer as the authorities introduce measures to control air pollution, for example strict checks on car exhaust emissions.

In this book we have learnt that the atmosphere protects the earth from meteorites and harmful radiation, that it regulates the temperature, and provides the oxygen and carbon dioxide necessary to support plant and animal life. We know it creates climate and weather patterns that farmers and others rely on. Left to itself, it would continue to provide these important services.

However, we have also learnt that humans are using the atmosphere as a huge rubbish dump for unwanted waste gases produced to support our way of life. These can be very unpleasant and even dangerous to breathe. More than that, they are changing the atmosphere and upsetting the delicate balance that has kept the world inhabitable for millions of years.

Some of the information you have read is undisputed scientific fact. For example, the amount of carbon dioxide in the atmosphere is increasing and the hole in the ozone layer does exist. These changes have been monitored and recorded by instruments. Other information is not so straightforward. The majority of scientists agree that acid rain damages trees, but some say it still remains to be proved. The problem is that a tree may be weakened by acid rain but killed by insects. In cases like this, you will have to make up your own mind who you think is right. You may realize you need more information before you can do this, in which case you can approach your teacher or your parents, visit the library or write to one of the organizations listed at the back of this book.

There are many predictions about what will happen if we continue to pollute the atmosphere in the way we are. They are based on studies of what has happened in the past. These predictions are very important because the action we decide to take, or not to take, will be based on them.

We have also learnt that we cannot take the environment for granted. All our activities change it, some for the better, some for the worse. Very often, we seem to forget that we are a part of nature and depend on it for everything. But there are limits to what it can provide, and when we try to push beyond these limits, we damage the environment.

It is now up to ~~you~~ us to consider what ~~you~~ we want to do. Are ~~you~~ we happy to go along with the world the way it is, or do ~~you~~ we want to change things? It is hoped that this book will have prompted you to think about one very important environmental issue and will help you decide what action you want to take.

One theory predicts that if the rate of global warming continues, the climate of northern Europe will become similar to that in Mediterranean countries.

Glossary

Acid A solution with a pH value of less than 7.0.

Acid rain Rain, snow and mist that has absorbed pollution in the atmosphere and become more acid.

Aerosol canister A container which holds liquids under pressure. The liquids are released in a fine spray through a nozzle.

Atmosphere The gaseous layer that surrounds the earth and is held there by gravity.

Catalytic converter A device fitted to car exhausts to remove pollution.

Chlorofluorocarbons (CFCs) The group of chemicals used in refrigerators and many aerosols which damage the ozone layer.

Climate The long-term, prevailing weather conditions.

Conservation Using resources in such a way that the environment is not damaged.

Convention An agreement made by a group of countries to work towards a common goal.

Dioxin A very poisonous industrial and agricultural chemical.

DNA, or deoxyribonucleic acid. An acid found in the cells of organisms. DNA passes on hereditary characteristics from parents to their offspring.

Ecosystem A community of plants, animals and other organisms and the environment in which they live and react to each other.

Emissions Substances discharged into the air from chimneys and vehicle exhausts.

Environment The surroundings in which all plants and animals live.

Environmental pressure group Groups like Friends of the Earth and Greenpeace which campaign for conservation and environmental action.

Fossil fuels Fuels obtained from organic substances, for example coal, oil and natural gas.

Global warming The increase in the average temperature of the earth caused by the build-up of greenhouse gases in the atmosphere.

Greenhouse gases The gases in the atmosphere which allow the heat of the sun to reach the earth, but slow down its escape.

Hydrocarbons Organic material composed of carbon and hydrogen. The basis of fossil fuels.

Nitrogen oxides (NOx) Gases formed mainly from nitrogen in the atmosphere when fuels are burnt at high temperature.

Organism Any animal or plant which can maintain life by itself.

Ozone (O3) A form of oxygen that can damage plant growth and irritate the eyes and breathing system, when it is concentrated near the surface of the earth.

Ozone layer A narrow layer of ozone found in the upper atmosphere. It filters out the harmful ultraviolet radiation of the sun.

pH The unit for measuring acidity.

Photo-electric cell A device for converting light into electricity.

Pollutants Substances which can damage the environment when released into it.

Pollution The presence in the environment of harmful substances called pollutants.

Predictions Forecasts of what is likely to occur in the future, based on scientific information.

Radiation In this book, radiation is the word used to describe the movement of energy from one place to another through space or the air. Some forms are dangerous to humans.

Radioactivity The radiation given off by certain materials.

Sulphur dioxide (SO2) A colourless gas with a strong odour formed primarily from burning fossil fuels.

Toxic waste Waste material that is poisonous.

Ultraviolet radiation Harmful, invisible light waves coming from the sun.

United Nations The international organization that brings all the countries of the world together to discuss and attempt to solve world problems.

Further reading

The Aerosol Connection Friends of the Earth (UK). Explains why we need the ozone layer and the threat to it from air pollution. Includes list of 'ozone friendly' aerosol products.

Air Ecology, Jennifer Cochrane (Wayland, 1987). One of a series looking at humans and the environment.

Air Pollution Pictorial Charts Educational Trust. One of a series of educational charts illustrating the major forms of air pollution.

Acid Rain World Wide Fund for Nature, 1988. A newspaper-style information sheet presenting the facts about acidification and what is being done to prevent it.

Campaign Briefings Greenpeace A series of short pamphlets on various environmental issues including air pollution.

The Gaia Atlas of Planet Management for today's caretakers of tomorrow's world (Gaia Books Limited) Maps and text to describe the state of the world today and how it can be kept healthy.

The Green Consumer Guide Gollancz A shopping guide that helps you choose products that are least damaging to the environment.

The Greenhouse Effect Friends of the Earth (UK) A poster-style sheet describing the causes, effects and solutions to global warming.

Lichens and Air Pollution BP Educational Service. Colour wallchart illustrating common lichens and how they indicate the level of air pollution in a given area.

Useful Addresses

Acid Rain Information Centre
Department of Environmental and Geographic
   Studies
Manchester Polytechnic
John Dalton Extension
Chester Street
Manchester M1 5GD
England

Collects information from concerned organizations in Britain and abroad. Postal enquiries answered if stamped self-addressed envelope included. There is also a speaker service, videos for hire and a display available.

Acid Rain Information Clearing House
Centre for Environmental Information Inc
33 S. Washington Street
Rochester
NY 14608
USA

Provides general information about acid rain.

Australian Association for Environmental Education
GPO Box 112
Canberra ACT 2601

CLEAR – Campaign for Lead Free Air
3 Endsleigh Street
London WC1H ODD
England

Campaigning organization which aims to remove lead from petrol and the environment.

Central Electricity Generating Board
Sudbury House
15 Newgate Street
London EC1A 7AU
England

Operates power stations and conducts research into all environmental problems connected with power generation. Publishes booklets, leaflets and films.

Friends of the Earth
26-28 Underwood Street
London N1 7JQ
England

An environmental pressure group which campaigns for conservation and environmental improvement. Publishes pamphlets and information packs.

Friends of the Earth (Australia)
National Liaison Office
366 Smith Street
Collingwood
Victoria 3065

Friends of the Earth (Canada)
Suite 53 54
Queen Street
Ottawa KP5CS

Friends of the Earth (NZ)
Nagal House
Courthouse Lane
PO Box 39/065
Auckland West

Greenpeace
30-31 Islington Green
London N1 8XE
England

An environmental pressure group campaigning for a cleaner and healthier environment. Produces informative booklets and posters.

National Society for Clean Air
136 North Street
Brighton BN1 1RG
England

Seeks to promote public education in all matters relating to the value and importance of clean air.

Sierra Club
730 Polk Street
San Francisco
CA 94109
USA

Publishes a regular newsletter with details of environmental legislation in the USA.

United Nations Environment Programme (UNEP)
PO Box 30552
Nairobi
Kenya

Produces UNEP News with up-to-date information on environmental issues.

World Wide Fund for Nature (International)
WWF Information and Education Division
1196 Gland
Switzerland

Produces information for education about acid rain.

Index

Picture acknowledgements

The publishers would like to thank the following for allowing their photographs to be reproduced in this book: Associated Press 28; Bruce Coleman Ltd 6 (Hans Reinhard), 10 below (Hans-Peter Merten), 11 (B & C Alexander), 12 (D Houston), 19 (Cliff Hollenbeck), 20 above, 25 below (L C Marigo); Geoscience Features cover; Greenpeace 35, 36; Hutchison Library 14 above (P Edward Parker), 22 (R Ian Lloyd), 24 (Caran McCarthy), 31 (Bernard Regent); ICCE 29 (Mike Hoggett); Oxford Scientific Films 25 above (Sean Morris), 37 below (Doug Wechsler), 37 above (Michael Leach); Photri 7, 10 above; Rex Features Ltd 33 above, 34 (Haley), 39 (Bradwell); Paul Seheult 40; Frank Spooner 27 (Julian Parker); Topham Picture Library 13, 14 below, 15, 20 below, 26, 39 left, 41 below; ZEFA 4 (Mueller), 5 (C Voigt), 21, 30, 33 below, 41 above (G Kalt), 42 (J O'Rourke), 43 (K Kerth). The illustrations are by Marilyn Clay.